I0820577

COLLEGE GOATs

THE GREATEST OF ALL TIME

GOATs OF COLLEGE WOMEN'S VOLLEYBALL

BY B. J. HOEPTNER EVANS

SportsZone
An Imprint of Abdo Publishing
abdobooks.com

abdobooks.com

Published by Abdo Publishing, a division of ABDO, PO Box 398166, Minneapolis, Minnesota 55439. Copyright © 2026 by Abdo Consulting Group, Inc. International copyrights reserved in all countries. No part of this book may be reproduced in any form without written permission from the publisher. SportsZone™ is a trademark and logo of Abdo Publishing.

Printed in the United States of America, North Mankato, Minnesota.
102025
012026

Cover Photo: Jamie Schwaberow/NCAA Photos/Getty Images
Interior Photos: UH Libraries, 5; Lyn Alweis/Denver Post/Getty Images, 6; Hawaii Athletics, 9, 14; Stanford Athletics, 10, 17; Pacific Athletics, 13; Long Beach State Athletics, 18, 22; Robert Beck/Sports Illustrated/Getty Images, 21; Tom G. Lynn/Time Life Pictures/Sports Illustrated/Getty Images, 25; John J. Kim/MediaNews Group/San Mateo County Times/Getty Images, 26; Brock Scott/NCAA Photos/Getty Images, 29; Peter Brouillet/Getty Images Sport/Getty Images, 30; Garry L. Jones/AP Images, 33; Hector Amezcua/Sacramento Bee/Tribune News Service/Getty Images, 34; Ryan McKee/NCAA Photos/Getty Images, 37; Elaine Thompson/AP Images, 38; Douglas Stringer/Icon Sportswire/Getty Images, 41; Jamie Schwaberow/NCAA Photos/Getty Images, 42

Editor: Dalton Rains
Series Designer: Kate Liestman

Library of Congress Control Number: 2025939138

Publisher's Cataloging-in-Publication Data

Names: Evans, B. J. Hoeptner, author.
Title: GOATS of college women's volleyball / by B. J. Hoeptner Evans
Description: Minneapolis, Minnesota: Abdo Publishing, 2026 | Series: College GOATs: the greatest of all time | Includes online resources and index.
Identifiers: ISBN 9781098298371 (lib. bdg.) | ISBN 9798384932178 (ebook)
Subjects: LCSH: College sports--Juvenile literature. | Women college athletes--Juvenile literature. | Volleyball--Juvenile literature. | Sports records--Juvenile literature. | College sports--Records--Juvenile literature.
Classification: DDC 796.325--dc23

TABLE OF CONTENTS

FLO HYMAN

Growing up in Los Angeles, California, Flora "Flo" Hyman sometimes felt self-conscious about her height. At 12 years old, she was already 6-foot-2. Some of her classmates teased her. However, things started to change when Hyman took up volleyball. She fell in love with the sport, and her height was a big advantage. On the court, her movements were graceful yet powerful. She could also let her competitiveness loose.

After high school, Hyman spent a year in junior college. The outside hitter transferred to the University of Houston in 1974. Now 6-foot-5, Hyman became the school's first female scholarship athlete. During her time in Houston, she lifted the Cougars to a pair of top-five national finishes. Meanwhile, she was named first-team All-American in each of her three seasons. In 1977, Hyman also earned national player of the year honors.

Hyman left Houston early in order to compete with the US Women's National Team. As team captain, she led the squad to the 1984 Olympics. Those Games were held in Los Angeles. The hometown crowd cheered from the stands as Hyman helped the team win a silver medal.

After the Olympics, Hyman went to Japan to play professional volleyball. However, her career came to a tragic end. Hyman was born with Marfan syndrome. People with that disorder are often tall. But Marfan syndrome also causes heart problems. Hyman died of a heart attack in the middle of a 1986 match. She was only 31 years old, but she left a lasting imprint on the sport.

Houston's Flo Hyman, *left*, leaps to return the ball.

Former USC setter Debbie Green competes with the US Women's National Team in 1980.

DEBBIE GREEN

Growing up in Southern California, Debbie Green knew that she didn't fit the mold of a typical volleyball setter. Setters often have to play at the front-right position on the court. Along with directing the ball, they often have to block opponents' best hitters. So setters are usually tall. At just 5-foot-4, Green was nowhere near the usual height.

When Green started playing at age 13, her small size was discouraging. But she didn't quit. She trained six days a week. She strengthened her legs so she could jump higher for blocks. She worked on making accurate passes to set up teammates.

The hard work paid off when Green arrived at the University of Southern California (USC) in 1976. As a freshman, she led the Trojans to a nearly perfect regular season. The team's only loss came against local rival University of California, Los Angeles (UCLA). Later that year, though, USC got a chance for revenge. At the time, women's college sports were part of the Association for Collegiate Athletics for Women (AIAW). USC and UCLA met in that year's AIAW championship game. This time, the Trojans came out on top to win the 1976 title.

Green didn't slow down the next year. The sophomore setter could often be heard shouting words of encouragement to teammates. She led USC to an undefeated regular season in 1977. The streak continued through the AIAW Tournament. By winning the title game, the Trojans became the first undefeated college volleyball champion. Green also earned national player of the year honors. She didn't win another championship with USC, but she later helped the United States win a silver medal at the 1984 Olympic Games.

DEITRE COLLINS

Volleyball wasn't Deitre Collins's first sport. Growing up in Los Angeles, California, she played several others before ever joining a volleyball team. In fact, she didn't become involved in the sport until her freshman year of high school. Deitre was the last player picked for the team. But she spent hours practicing and quickly improved.

College coaches didn't know much about Collins when she arrived at the University of Hawaii in the fall of 1980. But the 6-foot middle blocker soon got their attention. By the end of her freshman season, she was a starter for the Rainbow Wahine.

The young player only got better after that. In the summer of 1981, she traveled to Japan with her team. The Rainbow Wahine took part in exhibition matches there. Those games were more fast-paced than college competition. So Collins had to adapt. Her reflexes and decision-making skills got better.

Back in college, Collins sometimes felt as though the ball was moving in slow motion. As a sophomore in 1981, she recorded team highs with 433 kills and 40 solo blocks. That year, the National

FAST FACT

Collins's volleyball eligibility ran out after the 1983 season. However, she got to play on Hawaii's basketball team for the 1984–85 season. Playing at forward, she started 17 games and averaged 4.9 points and 6.0 rebounds per game.

Collegiate Athletics Association (NCAA) held its first women's volleyball tournament. The Rainbow Wahine made it to the Elite Eight.

In 1982, Hawaii faced USC in the national championship. The Rainbow Wahine dropped the first two sets. But Collins finished the match with 25 kills and helped the team come back to snatch the title.

Hawaii reached the championship game again in 1983. This time, the team swept UCLA for a second straight title. After the season, Collins was named the Collegiate Woman Athlete of the Year for all sports. It was the first time a volleyball player earned that award.

Hawaii middle blocker Deitre Collins was inducted into the American Volleyball Coaches Association Hall of Fame in 2008.

Middle blocker Kim Oden set a Stanford record with 665 career blocks.

KIM ODEN

In the 1980s, college volleyball was dominated by three sisters. The oldest was Kim Oden. Her strength and competitive spirit made her a standout at her California high school. By Oden's senior year, she had earned a reputation as one of the best volleyball players in the country.

Oden made an impact as soon as she arrived at Stanford in 1982. The 6-foot-2 middle blocker controlled games at the net with her quick reactions and powerful strikes. She lifted Stanford to a Final Four appearance in the 1982 NCAA Tournament. The Cardinal reached the semifinals again in 1983. However, they fell to Hawaii both years.

By her junior year, Oden was one of the most feared players in the nation. In the 1984 NCAA Tournament, Stanford finally broke through in the Final Four. The Cardinal beat the University of the Pacific 3–0. Although her team fell to UCLA 3–2 in the title game, Oden still earned national player of the year honors.

During Oden's senior year, Stanford once again met Pacific in the NCAA Tournament. This time, it was in the championship game. Oden's younger sister, Elaina, was a freshman at Pacific. The Cardinal suffered another title game loss. But the eldest Oden sister earned national player of the year honors for the second year in a row.

After college, Oden joined the US Women's National Team. She was team captain during the 1988 Olympic Games in Seoul, South Korea, and the 1992 Olympic Games in Barcelona, Spain. She earned a bronze medal in 1992. Later, she worked on the coaching staffs of several colleges.

ELAINA ODEN

Elaina Oden was the second of the three Oden sisters. As the middle child, she often found ways to stand out. Kim and Bev Oden both played at Stanford. But Elaina decided to play at the University of the Pacific in Stockton, California.

The second of the Oden sisters was a 6-foot-1 middle blocker. She had excellent vision and always seemed to be aware of the whole court. She was also a tireless worker, constantly learning new skills. As a freshman at Pacific, Oden recorded a .380 hitting percentage. That set the program's single-season record. In the 1985 NCAA Tournament, Oden led the Tigers all the way to the title game. She faced her older sister, Kim, and powerhouse Stanford. Pacific won 3–1. It was the school's first championship in any sport.

Oden led Pacific to another tournament run in 1986. The Tigers dominated the competition on their way to the title game. The championship was held at their home arena. Oden played an efficient game in front of the standing-room-only crowd. Her hits often found their way past opponents. She helped Pacific sweep Nebraska for the program's second straight title.

FAST FACT

In the 1992 Olympics, Kim and Elaina Oden went from opponents to teammates. The sisters lifted the US Women's National Team to a bronze medal. Four years later, Elaina and her younger sister, Bev, teamed up at the 1996 Olympics.

Oden missed the 1987 season due to a knee injury. She was back in 1988. The Tigers couldn't break through for Oden's third championship. But Oden ended her career as the most decorated player in Pacific's history.

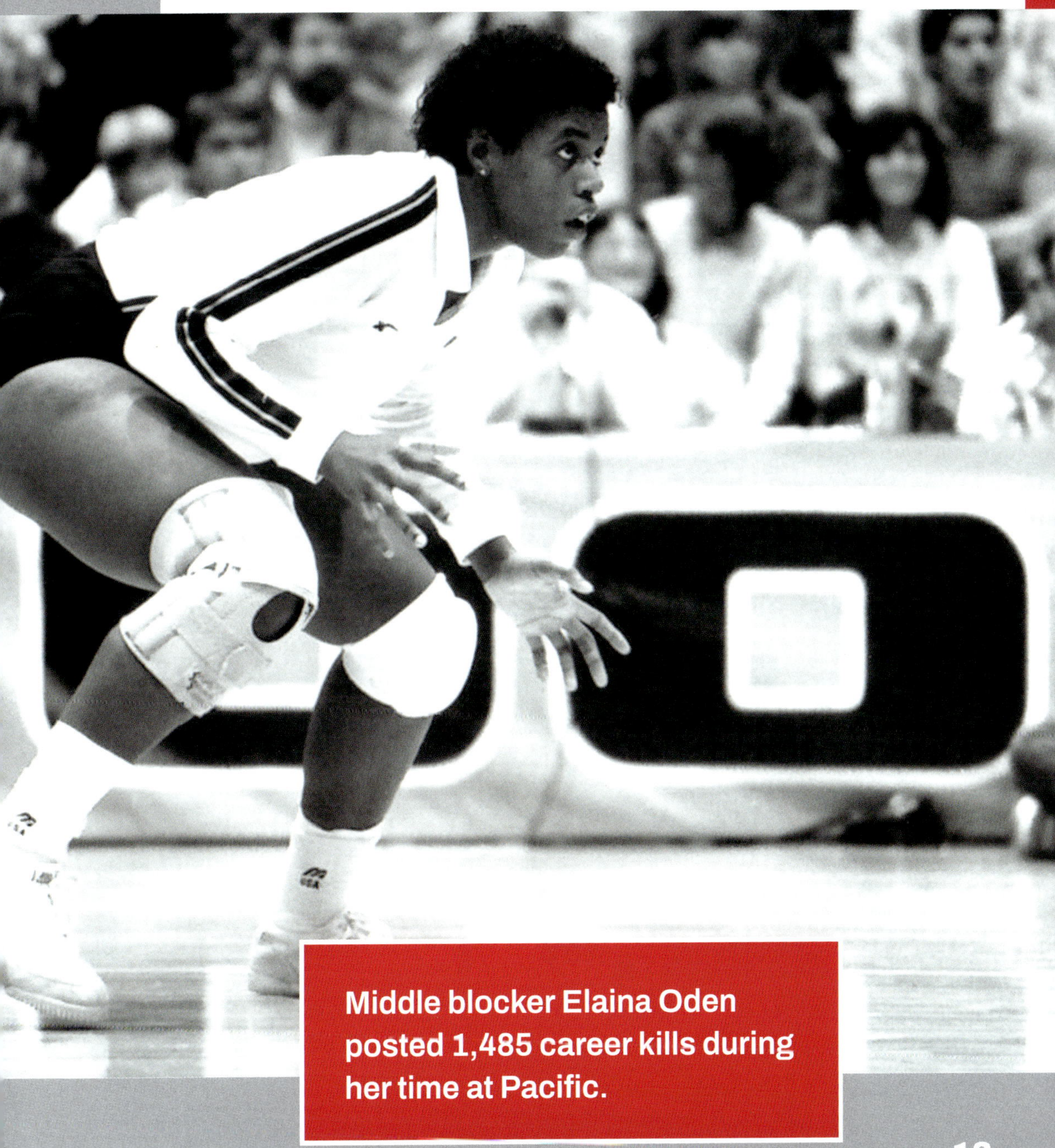

Middle blocker Elaina Oden posted 1,485 career kills during her time at Pacific.

Hawaii outside hitter Teee Williams piled up 1,873 kills and 1,143 digs in college.

TEEE WILLIAMS

Tonya "Teee" Williams was known for her powerful hits. Fans learned to expect searing spikes whenever the Hawaii star made contact. Williams's hits sometimes even drew blood from her opponents.

However, Williams did not rely on raw strength alone. The outside hitter also had extraordinary levels of endurance. Her shoulder never seemed to get tired, allowing her to deliver one punishing hit after another. In one memorable game, Williams hit the ball 103 times and piled up 39 kills.

Williams had to sit out her freshman season at Hawaii. After that, she started all 107 matches of her college career. The Rainbow Wahine won 99 of them. As a sophomore in 1987, Williams powered the team to a 37–2 overall record. In that year's NCAA Tournament, Hawaii gave up only two sets on the way to a victory over Stanford in the title game. Williams earned national player of the year honors for her dominant season.

Williams led Hawaii to the title game again in 1988.This time, the Rainbow Wahine fell short of a championship. Then, in 1989, they lost to Long Beach State in the regional final. But their star senior still earned co–national player of the year honors. After leaving Hawaii, Williams joined the US Women's National Team. She helped the United States win a bronze medal at the 1992 Olympics.

BEV ODEN

Beverly "Bev" Oden was always more interested in school than sports. She dreamed of attending Stanford University. However, she knew that her parents couldn't afford the tuition. Getting a volleyball scholarship would give her a chance to study at the elite school. Even though volleyball wasn't her top interest, the youngest Oden sister still became one of the greatest players in the history of the sport.

Upon arriving at Stanford in 1989, Oden made an immediate impact. The 6-foot-2 middle blocker was named a first-team All-American as a freshman. Her sophomore year was even better. That year, she set a single-match record with 41 kills against UCLA. Previously, the record of 32 had been held by her sister Kim Oden. The younger Oden was named national player of the year for the 1990 season.

Two years later, Oden added even more to her family's legacy. As a senior in 1992, she led Stanford to its first-ever national

FAST FACT

Stanford's 1992 title win set Bev Oden apart from her older sisters. Kim had earned national player of the year honors, but she never won an NCAA championship. Meanwhile, Elaina snagged two titles with Pacific while failing to earn national player of the year honors.

championship victory. She also became the first Cardinal to be named a first-team All-American in each of her four years with Stanford. The Oden family's place in history was secure.

Middle blocker Bev Oden left Stanford with 1,753 kills and 650 blocks.

Outside hitter Tara Cross piled up 1,578 digs at Long Beach State.

TARA CROSS

In the late 1980s, Tara Cross led Long Beach State's legendary "Soul Patrol." The 6-foot outside hitter was one of five Black starters on the 49ers volleyball team. This made the team stand out at a time when many college volleyball teams had few Black players. The historic team brought the program new levels of success.

Cross and the 49ers peaked in 1989. The senior powered her team to a 32–5 record. In the NCAA Tournament, Long Beach State defeated No. 1 Hawaii to advance to the program's first Final Four. Cross didn't stop there. After helping the 49ers to a 3–1 semifinal victory, she recorded 20 kills in the championship game. The 49ers swept Nebraska to clinch Long Beach State's first NCAA title in any sport.

Cross finished her career as a four-time All-American while earning national player of the year honors in 1988 and 1989. The 49ers star graduated with an NCAA-record 2,767 kills. That sum included a Long Beach State–record 47 kills in a single match.

FAST FACT

After college, Cross became a decorated international player. She competed in four Olympic Games from 1992 to 2004. That made Cross the first US volleyball player to compete in four Games. She earned a bronze medal in 1992.

NATALIE WILLIAMS

In the early 1990s, people around the UCLA campus could always tell when Natalie Williams drove past. Her car's license plate read "NAT KNOS." That was short for "Natalie Knows." The phrase was inspired by another famous athlete. Bo Jackson, a star baseball and football player, popularized the slogan "Bo Knows." It was part of a Nike advertising campaign. Like Jackson, Williams was a two-sport athlete. In fact, she was the first woman to earn first-team All-America honors for both basketball and volleyball in the same year.

At 6-foot-2, Williams's size and strength made her a dominant outside hitter. She led UCLA to a national title in 1992. The sophomore earned NCAA Tournament Most Outstanding Player (MOP) honors for her efforts. The next year, she set a UCLA record by slamming 43 kills in a match. Then she earned another tournament MOP after leading the Bruins to a second straight title. Williams was also named national player of the year for the 1991 season.

The Bruins fell short of a title in 1992. But Williams still earned national player of the year for a second straight season. At the

FAST FACT

Williams failed to make the US national volleyball team before the 1996 Olympic Games. But four years later, she competed in a different Olympic sport. Williams helped the United States' basketball team take gold at the 2000 Games.

same time, she piled up stats on the basketball court. She averaged 20.4 points per game during her college career. After graduating, Williams went on to have a successful professional basketball career.

UCLA outside hitter Natalie Williams's 2,115 career kills was an NCAA record when she graduated in 1992.

DANIELLE SCOTT

Danielle Scott started her college career playing middle blocker for Long Beach State. Middle blockers are often among a team's tallest athletes. The size helps when playing close to

Danielle Scott (2) recorded 604 blocks during her time with Long Beach State.

the net. Meanwhile, shorter players in the back row must be able to make tough digs to prevent opponents from scoring. Taller players sometimes struggle to move quickly enough to play in the back row. Some people didn't think the 6-foot-2 Scott had the speed or skills to play in the back row.

By the end of her college career, Scott had proved the doubters wrong. She led Long Beach State to deep tournament runs in 1991 and 1992. In 1993, she lifted the team to a title and earned national player of the year honors. Scott ended her career as the all-time NCAA hitting percentage leader, with a career average of .421. She also piled up 1,778 kills and 693 digs.

Scott wasn't just adaptable on the volleyball court. The versatile athlete also played basketball for Long Beach State, and she even ran track for one season. She earned all-conference honors in basketball. That made her the first Big West athlete to earn all-conference honors for two sports in the same year.

FAST FACT

Scott participated in her first Olympics in 1996. She competed in her final Games in 2012. That made her the first volleyball player ever to compete at five Olympics. The United States earned two silver medals during that time.

MISTY MAY

Growing up in Southern California, Misty May was surrounded by volleyball. Her dad, Butch May, had played for the United States in the 1968 Olympics in Mexico City, Mexico. Both her parents still played beach volleyball for fun at the nearby Santa Monica Pier. One of Misty May's babysitters during those games was future indoor and beach volleyball legend Karch Kiraly, who went on to become a three-time Olympic gold medalist.

With so much exposure to the sport, May soon began to play volleyball herself. By the time she arrived at Long Beach State, she was a standout setter who was a master at creating scoring opportunities for teammates. The freshman's talent and competitive drive earned her the starting job in 1995. That season, she led the 49ers to the second round of the NCAA tournament.

May kept getting better. Her team got better, too. The next two seasons, Long Beach State won the Big West and advanced deeper into the NCAA Tournament. The 49ers reached the Elite Eight in 1997. May also earned national player of the year honors that season.

FAST FACT

After college, May—later known as Misty May-Treanor—went on to play in four Olympics and win three gold medals as a beach volleyball player. That made her one of the most decorated athletes in the sport's history.

May's hard work really paid off as a senior. She continued to build her playmaking and defensive skills. The improvements helped Long Beach State go 36–0 in 1998. The perfect season ended with a championship. May was named co-MOP of the tournament and earned national player of the year honors for the second time.

Long Beach State setter Misty May piled up 5,046 career assists.

KERRI WALSH

Kerri Walsh grew up in Northern California. As a kid, she got to be a ball girl during a volleyball match at nearby Stanford. That's when her dream of becoming a Cardinal began. Walsh later led her high school volleyball team to three state championships. Stanford offered the hitter a scholarship.

Kerri Walsh recorded 1,285 career digs at Stanford.

Walsh led Stanford through the 1996 NCAA Tournament. The first-year star often found open hitting lanes. In the championship game, the Cardinal took down Hawaii 3–0. Walsh was named tournament MOP.

As a sophomore in 1997, Walsh struggled with shoulder problems. But even injuries couldn't slow her down. She recorded a team-high 307 digs. The Cardinal met Pennsylvania State (Penn State) for the NCAA title game. Walsh piled up 14 kills and six blocks while lifting Stanford to its second straight championship.

Stanford fell to Texas in the Sweet 16 of the 1998 tournament. In 1999, Walsh led the Cardinal back to the title game. This time, they couldn't make it past Penn State. However, Walsh was still named co–national player of the year for the season.

By the end of her career, Walsh had become the first player in conference history with at least 500 blocks, 1,200 digs, and 1,500 kills. She was the second college volleyball player in NCAA history to be named a first-team All-American all four years.

FAST FACT

Walsh—later known as Kerri Walsh Jennings—became a legendary Olympic volleyball player. In the 2000 Olympics, she competed on the United States' indoor team. Then she won three straight gold medals in beach volleyball with Misty May-Treanor. In 2012, her fifth Olympic appearance, Walsh won bronze with April Ross.

LOGAN TOM

Outside hitter Logan Tom had a lot to live up to when she arrived at Stanford in 1999. Tom had taken up volleyball when she was 13 years old. By 14, she was competing with the US Youth National Team. At 16, she was competing with the older players on the US Women's National Team. When she wasn't competing with the nation's best players, she was dominating high school games in Salt Lake City, Utah. Her team won two state championships. By the time she arrived at Stanford, Tom had already been featured in *Sports Illustrated* magazine and on ESPN.

If she felt any pressure heading to college, the star outside hitter didn't show it. Tom lined up next to senior hitter Kerri Walsh. Together they helped the Cardinal reach the 1999 NCAA title game. However, a 3–1 loss to Penn State left Tom hungry for more.

Tom missed the first six weeks of her sophomore season while competing at the 2000 Olympic Games in Sydney, Australia. At 19, she was the youngest US Olympic volleyball player ever. The team finished fourth. Tom considered taking some time off after the Games, but she ended up returning to Stanford for the second half of the season. However, the team lost in the second round of the NCAA Tournament.

Tom played her entire junior year. Her all-around skills powered Stanford to a 2001 NCAA championship victory. That season, she earned national player of the year honors and was named MOP of the NCAA Tournament. In 2002, Stanford lost in the Final Four. But Tom ended her college career by earning national player of the year honors for the second straight year.

Outside hitter Logan Tom's career 5.02 kills per set was a Stanford record.

OGONNA NNAMANI

Ogonna Nnamani was born with asthma. The condition made breathing difficult. But Nnamani didn't let that stop her from competing in sports. In eighth grade, she started playing volleyball for her high school in Normal, Illinois. By her junior year, Nnamani was a

Outside hitter Ogonna Nnamani piled up a Stanford-high 2,450 career kills.

standout outside hitter. She ended her high school career by leading her team to consecutive state titles.

Nnamani's success continued at Stanford. In 2001, she had 10 or more kills in 31 of her 35 matches. The 6-foot freshman didn't slow down in the NCAA Tournament. She piled up 13 kills in the Elite Eight. She added another 19 in the national title game. The Cardinal rolled to a 3–0 victory over Long Beach State.

Nnamani helped Stanford reach the 2002 title game. But the team fell short against USC. In 2003, the Cardinal fell in the Sweet 16. After that season, Nnamani became only the second women's volleyball player to compete for the United States in the Olympics while still in college. Nnamani helped the United States finish fourth at the 2004 Games in Athens, Greece. She immediately returned to California to play her senior season at Stanford.

The Cardinal went into the 2004 NCAA Tournament as the No. 11 overall seed. Few expected the team to make a title run. However, Nnamani had other ideas. A close win in the second round took Stanford to the Sweet 16. After that, the Cardinal blasted through the competition. They swept Texas and Wisconsin and moved on to the Final Four, where they took down conference rival Washington 3–1. Finally, Nnamani ended her college career with a 3–0 sweep over Minnesota in the title game. She sealed the championship with her 29th kill of the game. That gave her an NCAA record of 145 for the tournament.

After the championship game, Nnamani was named the 2004 NCAA Tournament's MOP. She also won the Collegiate Women's Athlete of the Year for all sports. Four years later, she got another chance for an Olympic medal. This time, the United States won silver medal at the 2008 Games in Beijing, China.

SARAH PAVAN

Sarah Pavan grew up in Ontario, Canada. Raised by two volleyball coaches, she started playing the sport at 10 years old. At 14, she was invited to train with the Canadian Junior National Team. At 16, she became the youngest person ever selected for the Senior National Team.

Many US colleges recruited the 6-foot-5 right-side hitter. Pavan thought Lincoln, Nebraska, felt most like her hometown. She joined the Nebraska Cornhuskers in 2004. The team fell short of a title in Pavan's first two seasons. In 2004, they lost in the Elite Eight. One year later, they fell in the title game.

The 2006 Elite Eight looked like more of the same. Nebraska dropped to a 0–2 deficit against Minnesota, and it looked as though Pavan's junior season would come to another disappointing end. But then Pavan took control of the match. She finished with 20 kills and 11 digs as the Cornhuskers clawed back for a 3–2 win.

That year's title game was being held in Omaha, Nebraska. To the delight of the crowd, Pavan's game-high 22 kills lifted the Cornhuskers to a 3–1 victory. She earned tournament MOP. Later, Pavan was named the Collegiate Woman Athlete of the Year for all sports.

Nebraska fell short of an NCAA title in Pavan's final season, but she found more success after graduation. She hoped to compete in indoor volleyball at the Olympics. However, Canada failed to qualify for the 2012 Games in London, England. Paven switched to beach volleyball. She appeared in two Olympics. And in 2019, she won a beach volleyball world title.

Right-side hitter Sarah Pavan, *in white*, set a Nebraska record with 2,008 career kills.

Middle blocker Foluke Akinradewo finished college with a Stanford-record .446 career hitting percentage.

FOLUKE AKINRADEWO

Foluke Akinradewo's athleticism was hard to miss. One summer in high school, she was training with the US Junior National Team. While the team was testing players' vertical jumps, Akinradewo leaped higher than the machine could measure.

The Florida native did not even play volleyball until her sophomore year of high school. Unlike most top players, she never played for a volleyball club. Her high school's volleyball coach kept asking her to join the team, and she finally gave in. The athletic Akinradewo quickly developed into an elite player.

Akinradewo arrived at Stanford in 2005. It wasn't hard to find the middle blocker on the court. The 6-foot-3 star was easy to spot with her trademark protective goggles. Entering the NCAA Tournament, the Cardinal had high hopes. But things didn't go as planned. Stanford's run lost steam in the second round after Akinradewo hit a ball out of bounds. She felt she had lost the match for the team.

Stanford went on to appear in three straight national championship games. But the Cardinal lost each time. It wasn't Akinradewo's fault. She had 15 kills in the 2006 title game, 18 kills in 2007, and eight more in 2008. Akinradewo was named a first-team All-American all three years and won national player of the year in 2007. Her post-college career saw more success. She went on to win one gold, one silver, and one bronze medal at three Olympic Games.

MEGAN HODGE

Megan Hodge helped Penn State set a new standard for college volleyball. From August 2007 to September 2010, the Nittany Lions won 109 straight matches. Hodge competed in 102 of them. More often than not, the 6-foot-3 outside hitter played a starring role.

Hodge's career started strong in 2007. Penn State went 34–2 and won the national championship. The freshman recorded a team-high 4.60 kills per game. She ended the season as a first-team All-American and the NCAA Tournament's MOP.

Some observers called the 2008 Penn State squad the best ever. Led by the sophomore Hodge, the Nittany Lions went 38–0 that year. The team didn't lose a single set until the semifinals of the NCAA Tournament. After another Penn State national title, Hodge was again named the tournament's MOP.

Somehow, Hodge improved even more in 2009. She piled up kills all season. Once again, Penn State went undefeated and won the title. Hodge earned national player of the year honors. Her success even got her noticed outside of volleyball. She earned co–Collegiate Athlete

FAST FACT

Hodge played alongside plenty of talented players at Penn State. Outside hitter Nicole Fawcett earned national player of the year honors in 2008. Setter Alisha Glass and middle blocker Christa Harmotto both earned Olympic medals with the US Women's National Team.

of the Year honors for any sport, alongside University of Connecticut (UConn) basketball star Maya Moore. Hodge finished her college career with three national championship rings. She later added a silver medal to the collection at the 2012 Olympic Games.

Penn State outside hitter Megan Hodge racked up 2,142 career kills.

MICHA HANCOCK

Before she started her freshman year at Penn State, Micha Hancock wasn't sure which position she would play. Hancock grew up in Edmond, Oklahoma. In high school, she was an opposite hitter who sometimes played setter.

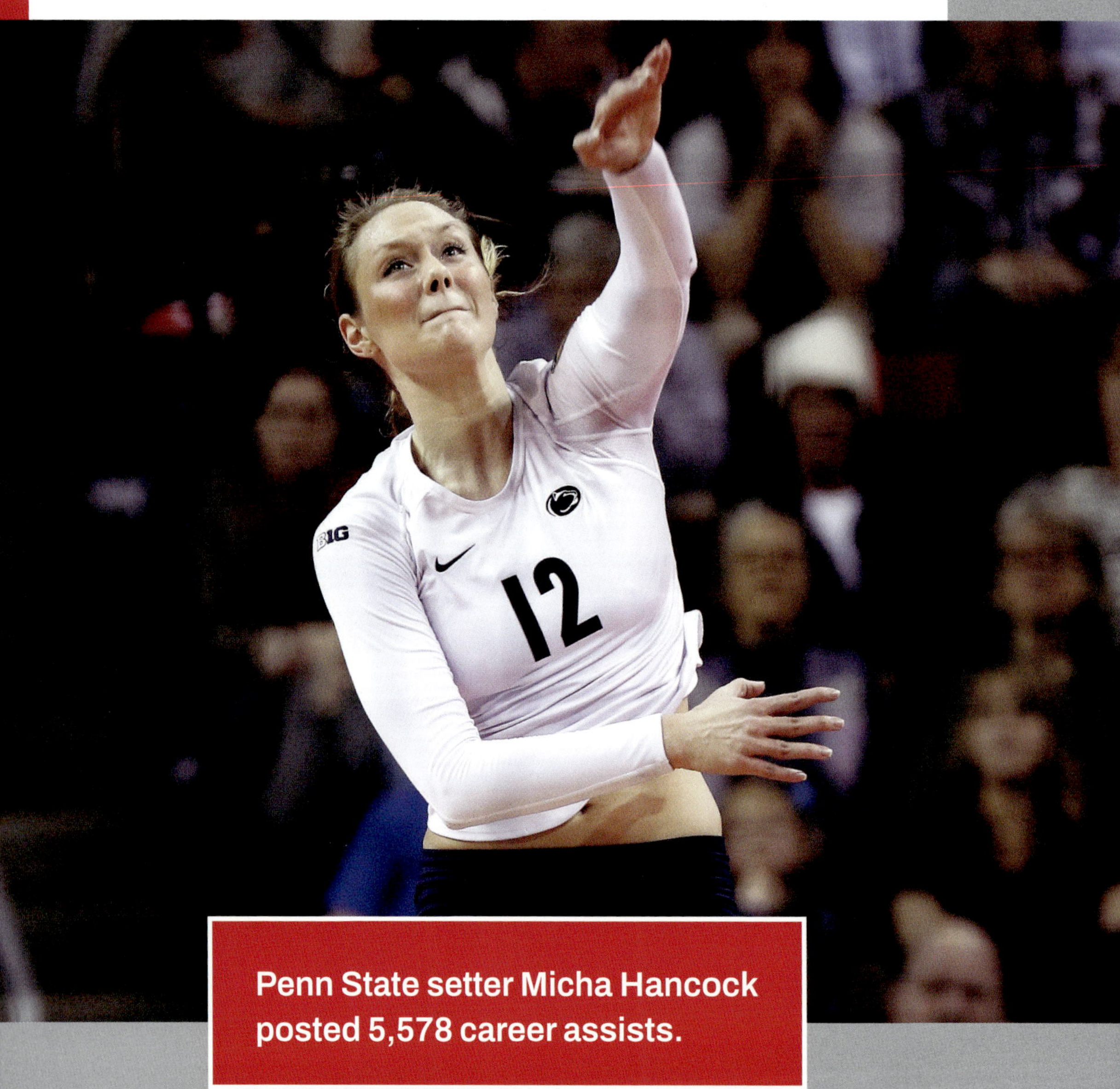

Penn State setter Micha Hancock posted 5,578 career assists.

Hancock was left-handed. Most teams are not used to seeing a left-handed opposite, which could have been an advantage for the freshman. However, that's not where she ended up playing. Before Hancock's second college match, coach Russ Rose made her Penn State's starting setter. She stayed there for the rest of her college career.

At the new position, Hancock was able to elevate her teammates. By 2012, the sophomore was known for her hard-to-return serves. After the regular season, she piled up an NCAA Tournament–record 22 aces. By the time she finished college, Hancock had set a Penn State record with 380 aces.

The 2013 season saw even more dominant play. That year, Hancock led the Nittany Lions to the NCAA title game. Facing Wisconsin, she recorded 48 assists, five kills, and three aces in a 3–1 victory. A year later, Penn State rolled to a second straight title game. Facing Brigham Young University, Hancock dished out 36 assists as the Nittany Lions pulled off a 3–0 sweep. The senior also earned national player of the year honors for her performance that season.

FAST FACT

Hancock went on to compete for the United States in the Olympics. After winning a silver medal in 2016, the team won gold in 2021. It was the US Women's National Team's first Olympic gold medal.

KATHRYN PLUMMER

Kathryn Plummer played lots of sports growing up, but she began to focus on volleyball when she was 10 years old. Even so, Plummer held on to her versatility, playing both indoor and beach volleyball. College volleyball programs started recruiting her when she was in seventh grade. The interest only grew as she got older.

By the time she arrived at Stanford, Plummer was 6-foot-6. She played indoor volleyball for the Cardinal, but her beach volleyball skills proved valuable during her freshman year. That season, Stanford's coach moved Plummer from opposite to outside hitter. While opposites can focus on hitting and blocking, outside hitters must also be good at passing and digging. Because of her time playing beach volleyball, Plummer had lots of experience with both skills.

Soon, Plummer was dominating the college volleyball world. From 2016 to 2019, she helped Stanford win three NCAA titles. She earned first-team All-America honors all four years. And she was named national player of the year in both 2017 and 2018.

FAST FACT

During the 2024 Olympic Games, Kathryn Plummer and her teammate Avery Skinner came in when the team needed hard hitters. The US Women's National Team's coach called them his "slugger lineup." The powerful duo helped the United States win a silver medal.

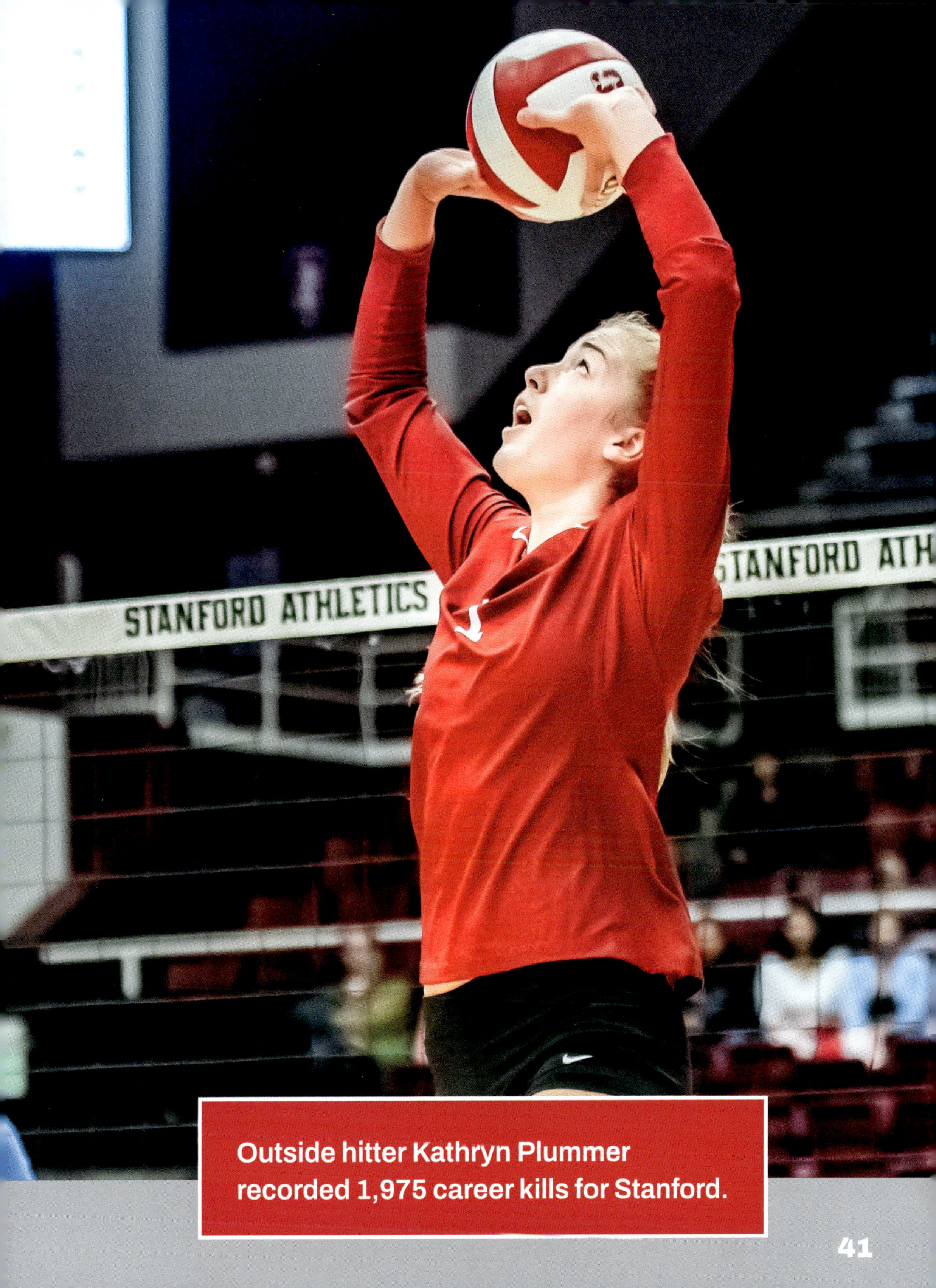

Outside hitter Kathryn Plummer recorded 1,975 career kills for Stanford.

Middle blocker Dana Rettke posted a Wisconsin-record 738 career blocks.

DANA RETTKE

At 6-foot-8, middle blocker Dana Rettke stood out on the court. In fact, she was the tallest Wisconsin player ever. But height alone does not make a volleyball player great. From the beginning, Rettke had to work hard to prove she belonged.

Because of her height, Rettke was often put in activities with older kids. Growing up in Illinois, she played both basketball and volleyball. To keep up with the more experienced players, she always had to work extra hard.

That attitude stayed with Rettke during her college career at Wisconsin. After her sophomore year, she was invited to compete with the US Women's National Team. Most of her US teammates had already graduated from college. Despite being one of the youngest on the team, Rettke was a key player as they won a gold medal at an international tournament in 2019.

Back in college, Rettke and the Badgers couldn't quite clinch a national championship. It wasn't because of Rettke. She was a first-team All-American in each of her first four years with the team.

Because of the COVID-19 pandemic, Rettke was allowed to play an extra college season in 2021. She took advantage of the opportunity. Rettke led the Badgers with 409 kills and 172 blocks for the season. Wisconsin finally broke through in the NCAA Tournament. The Badgers beat Nebraska 3–2 for the title. Rettke ended the season as national player of the year. Along the way, she became the first athlete in NCAA history to be named a first-team All-American five times.

HONORABLE MENTIONS

LAUREL BRASSEY IVERSEN

In 1974, Brassey Iversen became the starting setter for the defending NCAA champion San Diego State men's team. She was the first woman to play on a men's team. She later became the head coach of New Mexico's women's volleyball team.

RITA CROCKETT

Playing at Houston, Crockett was one of the best volleyball players of her era. The outside hitter was an All-American in 1977. Later, she won a silver medal at the 1984 Olympics.

ALLISON WESTON

Weston was a three-time All-American at Nebraska. In 1995, the middle blocker led the Cornhuskers to their first NCAA championship and was named co–Player of the Year. She later played for the US Women's National Team in the 2000 Olympic Games.

JORDAN LARSON

Larson, an outside hitter, left Nebraska with a career 127–8 record. Along the way, she led the Cornhuskers to the 2006 NCAA title. She later medaled at four Olympic Games and earned Most Valuable Player honors during the US women's gold-medal run in 2021.

MORGAN HENTZ

Hentz was a three-time first-team All-American with Stanford. Playing at libero, a position that focuses on defense and passing, she was also a three-time NCAA champion and was named co-MOP of the 2018 NCAA Tournament.

MADISEN SKINNER

Skinner won the 2020 national championship with Kentucky. The outside hitter then transferred to Texas, where she won two more titles in 2022 and 2023.

GLOSSARY

ace

A serve that lands in the opponent's court, scoring a point for the serving team.

block

A defensive action in which a player near the net stops an opponent from hitting the ball over.

dig

A defensive action in which a player prevents the ball from hitting the floor after an opponent spikes it.

eligibility

The ability to participate in a college sport.

endurance

Able to compete for long periods of time.

exhibition

A game that doesn't count in the standings.

hitting percentage

A statistic that tracks how successful a player is in converting attacks to points.

kill

An attacking hit that ends a rally and leads directly to a point.

pandemic

A widespread outbreak of a disease that affects a large portion of the population.

recruited

Convinced a high school athlete to join a college team.

scholarship

Money awarded to a student to pay for education expenses.

setter

A player who runs a team's offense and focuses on setting the ball to hitters.

spike

A hard-driven ball from a player's overhead swing that lands in the opponent's court.

versatile

Able to perform many different roles or functions.

MORE INFORMATION

BOOKS

Big Book of Who Women in Sports: The 101 Stars Every Fan Needs to Know. Triumph, 2025.

Price, Karen. *GOATs of Olympic Sports.* Abdo, 2022.

Stathes, Corbu. *Everything Volleyball.* Abdo, 2024.

ONLINE RESOURCES

To learn more about the GOATs of college women's volleyball, please visit **abdobooklinks.com** or scan this QR code. These links are routinely monitored and updated to provide the most current information available.

INDEX

ABOUT THE AUTHOR

B. J. Hoeptner Evans has worked in sports media and communications for more than 30 years. She dedicates this book to her husband, Bob, and son, Ben.